Write On, Mercy!

The Secret Life of Mercy Otis Warren

Gretchen Woelfle

Illustrated by Alexandra Wallner

CALKINS CREEK
Honesdale, Pennsylvania

To Carolyn P. Yoder, my esteemed editor
—GW

To all the good spirits of Casadrala, past and present: John, Ooty, Lodro,
Sang-gye, Ashe, Kiki, Taco, Winsor, and Newton
—AW

Acknowledgments

I would like to thank Louis Cataldo of Barnstable, Massachusetts, a peerless local historian,
for directing me to rewarding locations and resources early in my research.
The Massachusetts Historical Society was kind enough to send Mercy Warren's papers (on
microfilm) across the country so I could read thirty years of letters in Mercy's own hand. I am
grateful to Nancy Rubin Stuart for reading the final manuscript and for writing the definitive
The Muse of the Revolution: The Secret Pen of Mercy Otis Warren and the Founding of a
Nation. *Carolyn Yoder encouraged this project from start to finish. For this, her flawless*
editing, and ongoing friendship, she receives this book's dedication.
—GW

From her parlor window in West Barnstable, young Mercy Otis could watch the tide flow in and out of the Great Marsh on Cape Cod Bay. Spring brought warblers and snowy egrets flying north. Summer was the growing season, followed by autumn harvest, and winter nights by the fire. It seemed that Mercy's life would continue to quietly follow the seasons.

But it didn't.

Mercy learned to cook and spin, sew and embroider—useful skills. She learned to read and write—more rewarding. She and her six brothers and sisters listened to their father's political news from Boston. A traveling lawyer and later a member of the Massachusetts House of Representatives, James Otis helped make laws for the colony. The lawmakers might scrap like tomcats, but in the end they voted peaceably. That was democracy in action—and Mercy found *that* thrilling.

The family expected Mercy's oldest brother, Jemmy, to follow his father into politics. They expected Mercy, the oldest daughter, to marry and keep house like her mother.

But Mercy wanted more.

She was lucky.

Her father believed girls should learn along with boys—most fathers didn't. Studying with the local minister, Mercy and Jemmy read about ancient Greece and Rome, and English history, plays, and poems. Mercy's favorite book was *The History of the World* by Sir Walter Raleigh—full of stories of cruel kings and greedy leaders.

Jemmy went off to Harvard, but Mercy stayed behind. Girls couldn't go to college. So Jemmy brought his books home, and Mercy read John Locke's radical ideas of freedom and "natural rights."

Come leave the noisy smoky town
Where vice and folly reign,
The vain pursuits of busy men
We wisely will disdain.

True happiness and lasting peace
We ne'er in Courts can find
Ambitious views and sordid hopes,
By turns distract the mind.

But in the peaceful calm retreat
Amidst the beautious plains,
Where innocence with cheerful health
With love and virtue reign.

From "To J. Warren, Esq."
Mercy Otis Warren, 1766

Finally, Mercy went to Harvard—for Jemmy's graduation parties. She met his best friend, James Warren, with big brown eyes and a dimple in his chin. Not many men loved a smart woman, but James did, and Mercy loved him back.

James was a farmer and politician—like Mercy's father. Mercy kept house in Plymouth and raised five sons. But she had a secret life, too. When her children were asleep, she wrote poems. She didn't let her schooling fade away.

Life was quiet in Plymouth, but in nearby Boston, Samuel Adams and the Sons of Liberty were raising a ruckus. They rioted in the streets against taxes imposed by Great Britain. American colonists made their own tax laws, and they meant to keep it that way. Jemmy wrote fiery pamphlets about "natural rights" for men *and* women. Loyalists, Americans who sided with the British, railed against these "disloyal" Patriots.

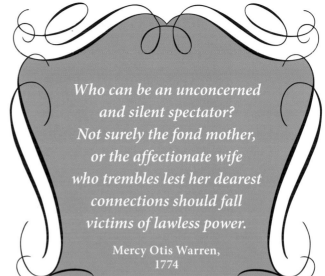

*Who can be an unconcerned
and silent spectator?
Not surely the fond mother,
or the affectionate wife
who trembles lest her dearest
connections should fall
victims of lawless power.*

Mercy Otis Warren,
1774

Soon Plymouth joined the clamor.
Mercy named her house "One Liberty
Square." Patriots met in the Warren
parlor to plan a Continental Congress
to unite the colonies against British
oppression. Most women would have
stayed out of sight, but not Mercy.
There she sat, speaking her mind,
loving the hubbub of politics.

Then . . . catastrophe! Jemmy, a bold and brilliant hothead, was savagely beaten by Loyalist enemies. Mercy cried, "Is it possible that we have men among us under the guise of officers of the Crown, who have become open assassins?" Jemmy's body healed, but his mind did not, and he was declared insane. The Patriots lost a great leader, and Mercy, her beloved friend.

To see the mind of a man
so superior thus darkened,
and that man
a most affectionate brother,
is grief beyond expression.

Mercy Otis Warren,
1773

Then more catastrophes! British troops marched into Boston. More riots . . . shots fired . . . five Americans lay dead . . . in what became known as the Boston Massacre.

Patriots refused to buy British goods. Mercy and her friends spun wool into thread, wove it with linen, and proudly wore "the Lindsey-Woolsey of their own Country"— not British cotton and silk.

But what *more* could Mercy do?

She could carry on Jemmy's work. Women didn't write about politics, but Mercy would change that.

Mercy's political plays appeared in Boston's papers. She cast her Patriot friends as heroes; her Loyalist enemies as villains—with names like Rapatio, Simple-Sapling, Crusty Crowbar, Hector Mushroom, and Hum Humbug. Patriots cheered. Loyalists raged—but they didn't know whom to blame.

*God has given you
great abilities. . . . For all these
I esteem I love you in a degree
that I can't express.
They are all now to be called into
action for the good of Mankind,
for the good of your friends,
for the promotion
of Virtue and Patriotism.*

James Warren, 1775

Mercy didn't sign her writing. Look what had happened to Jemmy. Also, people wouldn't respect a *woman* writer.

But a few people knew Mercy's secret—friends like John and Abigail Adams and her biggest fan, husband James.

They urged her to write on.

And she did.

Mercy wrote "The Squabble of the Sea Nymphs" about the Boston Tea Party—a night when Patriots dumped tea into Boston Harbor rather than pay a British tax. Her selfish nymphs sipped British tea, while patriotic Salacia poured it into the sea.

"Real genius," gushed John Adams.

Gazette JOURNAL of the Sea Nymphs

The fair Salacia, victory, victory, sings,
In spite of heroes, demi gods, or kings;
She bids defiance to the servile train,
The pimps and sycophants of George's reign.

From "The Squabble of the Sea Nymphs"
Mercy Otis Warren, 1774

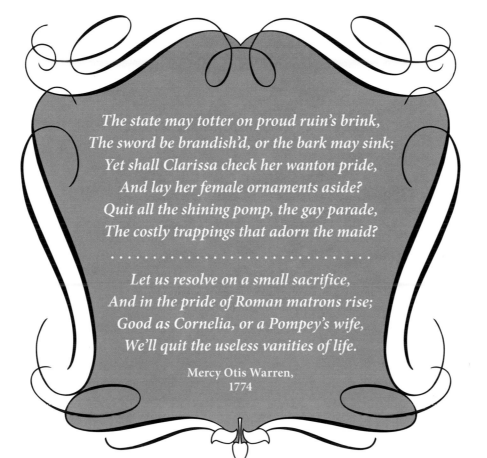

The state may totter on proud ruin's brink,
The sword be brandish'd, or the bark may sink;
Yet shall Clarissa check her wanton pride,
And lay her female ornaments aside?
Quit all the shining pomp, the gay parade,
The costly trappings that adorn the maid?

. . . .

Let us resolve on a small sacrifice,
And in the pride of Roman matrons rise;
Good as Cornelia, or a Pompey's wife,
We'll quit the useless vanities of life.

Mercy Otis Warren,
1774

Then all-out war! Battles near Boston at Lexington, Concord, and Bunker Hill! James joined George Washington's army as paymaster general. Mercy was torn between her husband and her sons. She worked as James's secretary at army headquarters. And at home, she packed her family's trunks, ready to flee if the British attacked.

Mercy still published political poems, but she wanted to do much more. She complained to Abigail Adams that men can attend "the great school of the world," while we "are confined to the narrow circle of domestic cares."

*Connected by nature,
friendship, and every social tie,
with many of the first patriots,
and most influential characters
on the continent; . . .
I had the best means
of information.*

Mercy Otis Warren,
1805

Mercy came up with her most ambitious plan yet—to write a history of the American Revolution. Men said history was too serious, too complicated for a woman. Mercy would prove them wrong.

And why not?

She shared her father's love of democracy, Jemmy's passion for freedom, and James's sense of duty. She had a fine education, a clever way with words, and "a mind that had not yielded to the assertion, that all political attentions lay out of the road of female life."

The war was still raging, but Mercy wasn't interested in battles. She wanted to write about people whose radical thoughts and bold actions aimed to banish a king and create a republic. People like her friends George Washington, Samuel Adams, John Adams, and dear Jemmy.

So, when she was nearly fifty, Mercy Otis Warren began her monumental work. Terrible headaches and eye infections plagued her. Her son James lost a leg in battle, and as she nursed him, she confessed, "the Muse [has] Grown too timid amidst the Noise of War."

Still she kept on. One, two, three sons died and she wrote, "the shaft flew thrice, and thrice my peace was slain." But her passion for politics survived. Mercy had a lot to say, and it took her thirty years to say it all, with husband James still cheering her on. By the time she finished, the war was long over and the United States of America was an independent republic.

*The waves
have rolled upon me,
the billows are repeatedly
broken over me,
yet I am
not sunk down.*

Mercy Otis Warren,
1800

Finally, in 1805, at seventy-seven, Mercy proudly signed her name
to three volumes—more than a thousand pages!—of . . .

*History of the
Rise, Progress and Termination
of the
American Revolution.*

*Interspersed with Biographical, Political
and Moral Observations.*

by Mrs. Mercy Warren

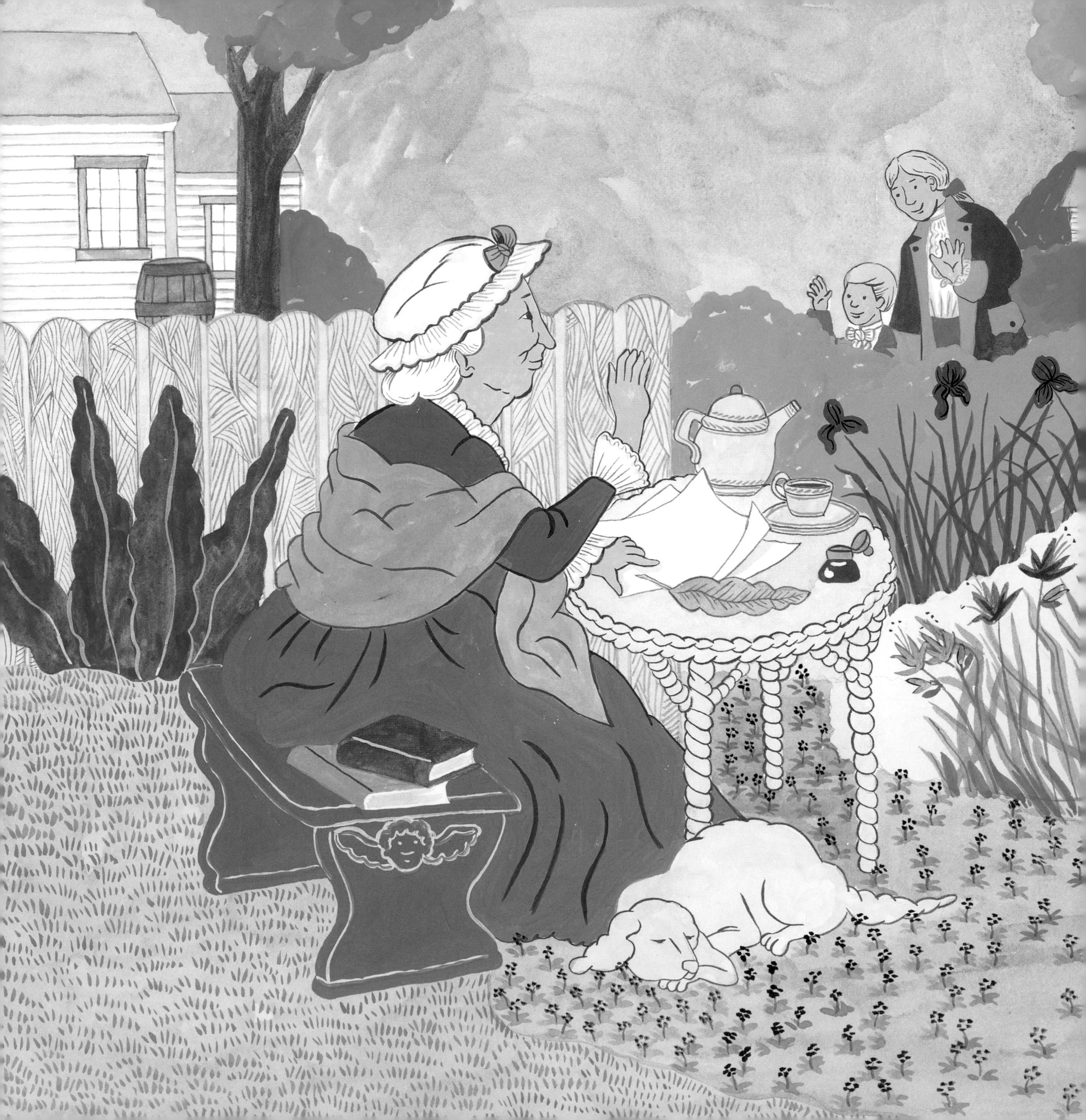

Her secret was out!
Mercy, write on!

Author's Note

Americans in the 1700s believed that men and women had separate spheres of influence: women in the home, and men in the outside world. Mercy pushed against these limits all her life. Men often considered women weak and frivolous, and Mercy agreed they sometimes were. But how could they be different when they had so few chances to develop their minds? Girls deserved as much education as boys!

In the decades after Mercy's death in 1814, more schools and even colleges were founded for girls. Educated women didn't stay in their "separate sphere" any more than Mercy did. They worked to end slavery, and in 1848 they gathered in Seneca Falls, New York, for the Women's Rights Convention. There they began the long campaign for the right to vote.

Mercy may not have dreamed of women as mayors, governors, and members of the U.S. Congress, but we can be sure she would be thrilled by it all.

Mercy Otis Warren posed for the famous American portrait painter John Singleton Copley around 1763, when she was in her midthirties. In the oil painting, she is fingering nasturtium vines, a symbol of patriotism. John Singleton Copley (1738–1815) painted many well-known Patriots—Paul Revere, John Adams, Samuel Adams, and James Warren, Mercy's husband, to name a few. Mercy's portrait was given to the Museum of Fine Arts in Boston by Winslow Warren, Mercy and James's great-grandson, where it remains today.

Mercy Otis Warren Timeline

1725   **James "Jemmy" Otis is born in West Barnstable, Massachusetts.***

1726   **James Warren is born in Plymouth, Massachusetts.**

1728   **September 14: Mercy Otis is born in West Barnstable, Massachusetts.**

1735   **Mercy begins studying with Jemmy and Rev. Jonathan Russell.**

1754   **Mercy marries James Warren; moves to Plymouth, Massachusetts.**

1757   **Son James Jr. is born.**

1759   **Son Winslow is born.**

1761   Navigation Acts are enforced. Jemmy argues against them and loses the case, but "American independence was then and there born," wrote John Adams.

1762   **Son Charles is born.**

1764   **Son Henry is born.**

1765   **James Warren elected to Massachusetts House of Representatives;** Stamp Act passed; Sons of Liberty threaten violence against those who pay the stamp taxes.

1766   **Son George is born;** Stamp Act repealed, but the British Parliament asserts power to make laws for the colonies.

1767   Townshend Acts place tax on paper, glass, and tea; large-scale boycott begins; women hold "spinning parties."

1768   British troops occupy Boston.

1769   **Brother Jemmy beaten in Boston coffeehouse.**

1771   **Jemmy declared insane.**

1772   **Mercy's *The Adulateur,* a patriotic play, published in Boston newspaper.**

1773   **Mercy's play *The Defeat* published in Boston, New York, and Philadelphia; Mercy meets Abigail Adams.**

1773   December 16: Boston Tea Party.

1774	**Mercy's "The Squabble of the Sea Nymphs" published;** Intolerable Acts limit Massachusetts self-government; port of Boston closed to trade; Continental Congress forms a loose national government.
1775	***The Group,* Mercy's third play, published in newspapers and as a pamphlet; more of her political poems published in newspapers.**
1775	April: Battle of Lexington and Concord; Congress creates the Continental army led by George Washington; **husband James becomes General Warren.**
1776	March 17: British troops leave Boston; July 4: American colonies declare independence from Great Britain.
1778	**"The Genius of America weeping for the absurd Follies of the Day," Mercy's political poem, published in Boston newspaper.**
1779	**Mercy's "Simplicity," another political poem, published in Boston.**
1781	Continental army defeats British army at Yorktown, last major battle of the war.
1783	**Jemmy killed when struck by lightning;** peace treaty signed with Britain.
1785	**Son Charles dies of tuberculosis.**
1790	**Mercy publishes the book *Poems Dramatic and Miscellaneous,* signed "Mrs. M. Warren."**
1791	**Son Winslow joins the army and is killed in Indian raid in Ohio.**
1800	**Son George dies of a fever.**
1805	***History of the Rise, Progress and Termination of the American Revolution* published in three volumes, signed "Mrs. Mercy Warren of Plymouth, Mass."**
1808	**Husband James dies.**
1814	**Mercy Otis Warren dies and is buried with James in the Old Burial Hill, Plymouth, Massachusetts.**

*****Bold milestones** refer to Mercy and her family*

Selected Bibliography

All quotations in this book come from the following sources:

Primary Sources

Adams Family Correspondence. 2 vols. Cambridge, MA: Belknap Press of Harvard University Press, 1963.

Otis, James. "The Rights of the British Colonies Asserted and Proved." In *Pamphlets of the American Revolution*, edited by Bernard Bailyn, 418–482. Cambridge, MA: Harvard University Press, 1965.

Warren, Mercy Otis. *History of the Rise, Progress and Termination of the American Revolution. Interspersed with Biographical, Political and Moral Observations. In Three Volumes.* 1805 edition. Boston: AMS Press, 1970.

———. *Mercy Warren Letterbook.* Boston: Massachusetts Historical Society, 1770–1800.

———. *The Plays and Poems of Mercy Otis Warren.* Delmar, NY: Scholars' Facsimiles and Reprints, 1980.

Warren-Adams Letters. 2 vols. Boston: Massachusetts Historical Society Collections, 1917–1925.

Secondary Sources

Fritz, Jean. *Cast for a Revolution: Some American Friends and Enemies, 1728–1814.* Boston: Houghton Mifflin, 1972.

Hayes, Edmund M. "The Private Poems of Mercy Otis Warren." *New England Quarterly* 54 (1981): 199–224.

Kerber, Linda K. *Women of the Republic: Intellect and Ideology in Revolutionary America.* Chapel Hill: University of North Carolina Press, 1980.

Norton, Mary Beth. *Liberty's Daughters: The Revolutionary Experience of American Women, 1750–1800.* Ithaca, NY: Cornell University Press, 1996.

Stuart, Nancy Rubin. *The Muse of the Revolution: The Secret Pen of Mercy Otis Warren and the Founding of a Nation.* Boston: Beacon Press, 2008.

Zagarri, Rosemarie. *A Woman's Dilemma: Mercy Otis Warren and the American Revolution.* Wheeling, IL: Harlan Davidson, 1995.

Books for Young Readers

Anderson, Laurie Halse. *Independent Dames: What You Never Knew about the Women and Girls of the American Revolution.* New York: Simon and Schuster, 2008.

Aronson, Marc. *The Real Revolution: The Global Story of American Independence.* New York: Clarion Books, 2005.

Bober, Natalie. *Countdown to Independence: A Revolution of Ideas in England and Her American Colonies: 1760–1776.* New York: Atheneum, 2001.

Gillis, Jennifer Blizin. *Mercy Otis Warren: Author and Historian.* Minneapolis: Compass Point Books, 2006.

Zeinert, Karen. *Those Remarkable Women of the American Revolution.* Brookfield, CT: Millbrook Press, 1996.

Websites[*]

David Lewis, Sculptor. **dlewis-sculpture.com**
Website of artist David Lewis, creator of the sculptures of Mercy Otis Warren and James Otis that stand in front of the county courthouse in Barnstable, Massachusetts.

History of American Women Blog
womenhistoryblog.com/2008/11/mercy-otis-warren.html
Describes Mercy and other important women in early America.

Museum of Fine Arts, Boston. **mfa.org**
Under "Collections," search "John Singleton Copley" to view the artist's portraits of James Warren and Mrs. James Warren (Mercy Otis Warren), among others.

Pilgrim Hall Museum. **pilgrimhall.org/mercytable.htm**
Mercy was adept with a needle as well as a pen. The Pilgrim Hall Museum in Plymouth, Massachusetts, owns a stunning embroidered tabletop made by Mercy, a photo of which is shown on the site.

Tales of Cape Cod. **talesofcapecod.org**
The Mercy Otis Warren Woman of the Year Award, sponsored by the Tales of Cape Cod organization, is given each year to a Cape Cod resident who has shown leadership in the community and has embraced the ideals of patriotism.

*Websites active at time of publication

Calkins Creek
An Imprint of Boyds Mills Press, Inc.
815 Church Street
Honesdale, Pennsylvania 18431
Printed in China

ISBN: 978-1-59078-822-6

Library of Congress Control Number: 2011917495

First edition

The text of this book is set in Minion.
The illustrations are done in Winsor & Newton gouache.

10 9 8 7 6 5 4 3 2 1